Only One of Me

Selected by
Helen Cook and
Morag Styles

Illustrated by
Tamara Capellaro
Carey Bennett and
Caroline Holden

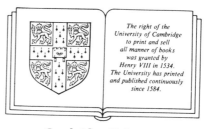

The right of the
University of Cambridge
to print and sell
all manner of books
was granted by
Henry VIII in 1534.
The University has printed
and published continuously
since 1584.

Cambridge University Press

Cambridge
New York   Port Chester
Melbourne   Sydney

Published by the Press Syndicate of the University of Cambridge
The Pitt Building, Trumpington Street, Cambridge CB2 1RP
40 West 20th Street, New York, NY 10011-4211, USA
10 Stamford Road, Oakleigh, Melbourne 3166, Australia

First published 1991

Printed in Great Britain at the University Press, Cambridge

British Library cataloguing in publication data
Only One of Me.
1. Poetry in English – Anthologies
I. Cook, Helen 1954–   II. Styles, Morag
821.008

ISBN 0 521 39060 5

Contents

Come Rock with I

Come Rock
With I

$

A one a two a one two three four –
boogie woogie chou chou cha cha chatta
noogie. Woogie wop a loo bop a wop
bim bam. Da doo ron a doo ron oo wop a
sha na? Na na hey hey doo wah did.
Um, didy ay didy shala lala lala lala,
boogie woogie choo choo cha cha bop.
(A woogie wop a loo bam) yeah yeah yeah.

Carol Ann Duffy

I'm a Hip Hoppy Kid

I'm a hip hoppy kid and you'll never catch me nappin,
No matter where I go you'll always hear me rappin . . .
I rap to the east and I rap to the west . . .
I rap in my socks and I rap in my vest . . .
I rap in my sleep and drive the neighbours potty . . .
I rap in the bathroom when I'm drying off my botty . . .
I rap to the birds and I rap to the bees . . .
And when I go completely daft I rap to the trees . . .
I can even rap on wheels, I really am the master . . .
I wish I'd seen that manhole then I wouldn't be in plaster . . .

Kirtiss Horswell (aged 9)

Well Listen

Well listen,
Well listen,
Well listen,

I want all
Dance fan
Folla dis instruction

Well jus ease
Off a de clutch
Likkle bit
Right leg slide in,
Now go down
Pon exhellarata
And push,
Go inna second
Gear and ease
Your body over
To de lef,
Now rush fe
Reach fort gear
And whine.

I want all
Dance fan
Folla dis instruction

Well listen,
Well listen,
Well listen.

Kendall Smith

Beat Drummers

Come Zipporah come rock with I
songs of praise to set spirit high,
drummers beat drummers beat,
we were never here to stay
hear that sound from far away,
drummers beat, drummers beat,
beat drummers beat 'cause the beat well sweet
beat down the beat that cools the heat,
drummers beat, drummers beat.

Come little children rock with I
the beat of the drum will never die,
drummers beat, drummers beat,
drum beat sound will never drown
listen to the beat as the beat beats a hard,
drummers beat, drummers beat
beat drummers beat and beat it hard
beat it like you beat and when you beat it back a yard,
drummers beat, drummers beat,
beat drummers, beat drummers beat drummers beat.

Benjamin Zephaniah

EXTRACT FROM **Drums**

Drums drums drums
The gods laughed
And it roared with thunder
Man rejoiced and clapped
Led by the drummer

Lari Williams

Way Down in the Music

I get way down in the music
Down inside the music
I let it wake me
       take me
Spin me around and make me
Uh-get down

Inside the sound of the Jackson Five
Into the tune of Earth, Wind and Fire
Down in the bass where the beat comes from
Down in the horn and down in the drum
I get down
I get down

I get way down in the music
Down inside the music
I let it wake me
       take me

Spin me around and shake me
I get down down
I get down

Eloise Greenfield

EXTRACT FROM **Didn't He Ramble**

Bring me now where the warm wind
blows, where the grasses
sigh, where the sweet
tongue'd blossom flowers

where the showers
fan soft like a fisherman's
net thrown through the sweet-
ened air

Bring me now where the workers
rest, where the cotton drifts,
where the rivers are
and the minstrel sits

on the logwood stump
with the dreams of his slow guitar.

Edward Kamau Brathwaite

What the Wind Said

'Far away is where I've come from,' said the wind.
'Guess what I've brought you.'
    'What?' I asked.
'Shadows dancing on a brown road by an old
Stone fence,' the wind said. 'Do you like that?'
    'Yes,' I said. 'What else?'
'Daisies nodding, and the drone of one small airplane
In a sleepy sky,' the wind continued.
    'I like the airplane, and the daisies too,' I said.
    'What else!'
'That's not enough?' the wind complained.
    'No,' I said. 'I want the song that you were singing.
    Give me that.'
'That's mine,' the wind said. 'Find your own.' And left.

Russell Hoban

A Minor Bird

I have wished a bird would fly away,
And not sing by my house all day;

Have clapped my hands at him from the door
When it seemed as if I could bear no more.

The fault must partly have been in me.
The bird was not to blame for his key.

And of course there must be something wrong
In wanting to silence any song.

Robert Frost

The Twelve Days of Christmas

On the first day of Christmas
My true love sent to me
A cornbird in a palm tree.

On the second day of Christmas
My true love sent to me
Two coconuts,
And a cornbird in a palm tree.

On the third day of Christmas
My true love sent to me
Three pastelles,
Two coconuts,
And a cornbird in a palm tree.

20

On the fourth day of Christmas
My true love sent to me
Four pumpkin pies,
Three pastelles,
Two coconuts,
And a cornbird in a palm tree.

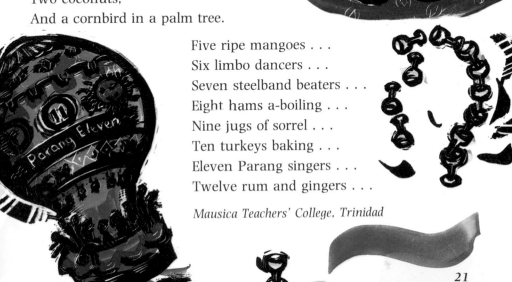

Five ripe mangoes . . .
Six limbo dancers . . .
Seven steelband beaters . . .
Eight hams a-boiling . . .
Nine jugs of sorrel . . .
Ten turkeys baking . . .
Eleven Parang singers . . .
Twelve rum and gingers . . .

Mausica Teachers' College, Trinidad

Three Owls in a Wood

There once were three owls in a wood
Who always sang hymns when they could:
What the words were about
One could never make out,
But one felt it was doing them good.

Anon

EXTRACT FROM **I Cannot Give the Reasons**

I cannot give the reasons,
I only sing the tunes:
the sadness of the seasons
the madness of the moons.

Mervyn Peake

A Cockney Alphabet

A 'Ay for 'orses

B Beef or mutton

C Seaforth Highlanders

D Deef or dumb

E 'Eave a brick

F Effervescence

G Chief of Police

H 'Ate ye for it

I 'Igh falutin'

J Jaffa oranges

K Cafe for a cuppa

L 'Ell for leather

M Emphasis

N 'En for eggs

O Over my dead body

P Pee for a penny

Q Queue for the flicks

R 'Alf a mo'

S As for you . . .

T Tea for two

U Euphemism

V Vive la France

W Double you for a pound

X Eggs for breakfast

Y Wife or girlfriend?

Z 'S head for 'is 'at.

Traditional

Song for a Banjo Dance

Shake your brown feet, honey,
Shake your brown feet, chile,
Shake your brown feet, honey,
Shake 'em swift and wil' –
  Get way back, honey,
  Do that rockin' step.
  Slide on over, darling,
    Now! Come out
    With your left.
Shake your brown feet, honey,
Shake 'em honey chile.

Sun's going down this evening –
Might never rise no mo'.
The sun's going down this very night –
Might never rise no mo'
So dance with swift feet, honey,
  (The banjo's sobbing low)
Dance with swift feet, honey –
  Might never dance no mo'.

Shake your brown feet, Liza,
Shake 'em, Liza, chile,
Shake your brown feet, Liza,
  (The music's soft and wil')
Shake your brown feet, Liza,
  (The banjo's sobbing low)
The sun's going down this very night –
Might never rise no mo'.

Langston Hughes

Drum Feet
(The origins of tap dancing)

Step, hop, flap, drop,
Long march from the forest to the farm.
Jump, heel-dig, ball-dig, stomp
We danced when they took away our drums.

Spring, ripple, back-brush, scuff,
Toe-beat, ball-beat, pick-up, riff.
Straight-tap, forward-tap, ball-tap, heel-tap,
Toe-tap, back-tap, pull-back, stamp.

Stormy and sick, scorning the whip.
Limboed when they chained us to the hull.
Pride in defeat. Wise in the street,
Talking to our brothers through the rhythms of our feet.

Jump, heel-dig, ball-dig, stomp,
Louder than the whiplash or the gun.
Straight-tap, forward-tap, pull-back, stamp,
We danced when they took away our drums.

Mike Taylor

Black Bottom

We're practising for the school show
I'm trying to do the Cha Cha and the Black Bottom
but I can't get the steps right
my right foot's left and my left foot's right
my teacher shouts from the bottom
of the class, come on show

us what you can do – I thought
you people had it in your blood.
My skin is hot as burning coal
like that time she said Darkies are like coal
in front of the whole class – my blood?
what does she mean? I thought

she'd stopped all that after the last time
my dad talked to her on parents' night
the other kids are allright till she starts
my feet step out of time, my heart starts
to miss beats like when I can't sleep at night
What Is In My Blood? The bell rings. It is time.

Jackie Kay

When I Dance

When I dance it isn't merely
That music absorbs my shyness,
My laughter settles in my eyes,
My swings of arms convert my frills
As timing tunes my feet with floor
As if I never just looked on.

It is that when I dance
O music expands my hearing
And it wants no mathematics,
It wants no thinking, no speaking,
It only wants all my feeling
In with animation of place.

When I dance it isn't merely
That surprises dictate movements,
Other rhythms move my rhythms,
I uncradle rocking-memory
And skipping, hopping and running
All mix movements I balance in.

It is that when I dance
I'm costumed in a rainbow mood,
I'm okay at any angle,
Outfit of drums crowds madness round,
Talking winds and plucked strings conspire,
Beat after beat warms me like sun.

When I dance it isn't merely
I shift bodyweight balances
As movement amasses my show,
I celebrate each dancer here,
No sleep invades me now at all
And I see how I am tireless.

It is that when I dance
I gather up all my senses
Well into hearing and feeling,
With body's flexible postures
Telling their poetry in movement
And I celebrate all rhythms.

James Berry

Happiness

An empty bus
hurtles through the starry night.
Perhaps the driver is singing,
and is happy because he sings.

Günther Grass

The One about Fred Astaire

No

it's
    not so much
        how

he
    moves so much
     so much
      as how he
      stops

and then moves so
  much again all
    over
      every
        anywhere
      all over
        so much

thank you
    Mister Astaire

so much

Adrian Mitchell

Klassical Dub

dis is a dreadful bad bass bounce
blood a leap an pulse a pounce

riddim cuttin sharp
riddim cuttin sharp
riddim cuttin sharp so

whatta search mi riddim on de hi-fi
whatta dreadful bounce heavy-low
whatta jucky-jucky-jucky-jucky juck-ee

jucky-jucky bounce
jucky-jucky bounce
jucky-jucky bounce

blast an tumble rumblin doun soh!

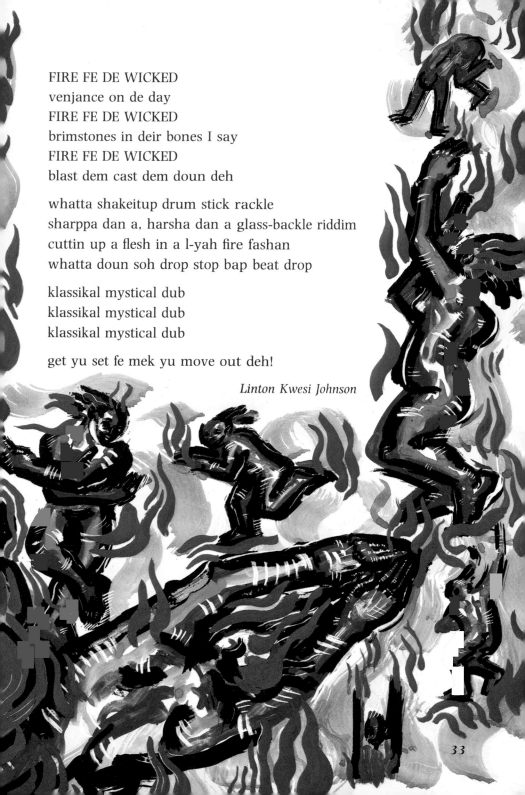

FIRE FE DE WICKED
venjance on de day
FIRE FE DE WICKED
brimstones in deir bones I say
FIRE FE DE WICKED
blast dem cast dem doun deh

whatta shakeitup drum stick rackle
sharppa dan a, harsha dan a glass-backle riddim
cuttin up a flesh in a l-yah fire fashan
whatta doun soh drop stop bap beat drop

klassikal mystical dub
klassikal mystical dub
klassikal mystical dub

get yu set fe mek yu move out deh!

Linton Kwesi Johnson

Break/dance

I'm going to break/dance
turn rippling glass
stretch my muscles
to the bass

Whoo!

I'm going to break/dance
I'm going to rip it
and jerk it
and take it apart

I'm going to chop it
and move it
and groove it

Ooooooh I'm going to ooze it
electric boogaloo
electric boogaloo
across your floor

I'm going to break/dance
watch my ass
take the shine
off your laugh

Whoo!

I'm going to dip it
and spin it
let my spine twist it
Ooooh I'm going to shift it
and stride it
let my mind glide it

Then I'm going to ease it
ease it
and bring it all home
all home
          believing in the beat
          believing in the beat
          of myself

Grace Nichols

Where the Rainbow Ends

Where the rainbow ends
There's going to be a place, brother,
Where the world can sing all sorts of songs,
And we're going to sing together, brother,
You and I, though you're white and I'm not.
It's going to be a sad song, brother,
Because we don't know the tune,
And it's a difficult tune to learn,
But we can learn, brother, you and I.
There's no such tune as a black tune.
There's no such tune as a white tune.
There's only music, brother,
And it's music we're going to sing
Where the rainbow ends.

Richard Rime

Take Me
Like I Am

Me and the Mule

My old mule,
He's got a grin on his face.
He's been a mule for so long
He's forgot about his race.

I'm like that old mule –
Black – and don't give a damn!
You got to take me
Like I am.

Langston Hughes

Before and After

Before I was alive
I wasn't anywhere.

I wasn't inside a mother
I wasn't a voice in the dark
I wasn't a movement in a room
I wasn't in a locked box
I wasn't under a pillow

I was utterly nowhere
I had no place
no space
no mark
no beginning
there was no me
there was only a nothing

and then again
I won't be inside a mother
I won't be a voice in the dark
I won't be a movement in a room
I won't be in a locked box
I won't be under a pillow

and the nothing
was full of other people
who didn't even know
that I was a nothing.

When I die
I won't be anywhere
I will give myself
to medical students
to cut up into bits
so that they can try and remember
where the bits go
and then they can throw the bits
in a bin
and burn the bits
and send the ashes off
to somewhere they're filling
in a bit of wet land

I'll be utterly nowhere
I will have no place
no space
no mark
no beginning
there will be no me
there'll only be a nothing

and the nothing
will be full of people
who won't even know . . .
No!
who *might* know . . .
who?

Michael Rosen

Infant Sorrow

My mother groand! my father wept.
Into the dangerous world I leapt:
Helpless, naked, piping loud:
Like a fiend hid in a cloud.

Struggling in my father's hands:
Striving against my swadling bands:
Bound and weary I thought best
To sulk upon my mother's breast.

William Blake

Conversation with Myself

This face in the mirror
stares at me
demanding, *Who are you? What will you become?*
and taunting, *You don't even know.*
Chastened, I cringe and agree
and then
because I'm still young,
I stick out my tongue.

Eve Merriam

Who Are You?

I'm Nobody! Who are you?
Are you – Nobody – too?
Then there's a pair of us?
Don't tell! they'd advertise – you know!

How dreary – to be – Somebody!
How public – like a Frog –
To tell one's name – the livelong June –
To an admiring Bog!

Emily Dickinson

Somebody

Somebody being a nobody,
Thinking to look like a somebody,
Said that he thought me a nobody:
Good little somebody-nobody,
Had you not known me a somebody,
Would you have called me a nobody?

Alfred, Lord Tennyson

One

Only one of me
and nobody can get a second one
from a photocopy machine.

Nobody has the fingerprints I have.
Nobody can cry my tears, or laugh my laugh
or have my expectancy when I wait.

But anybody can mimic my dance with my dog.
Anybody can howl how I sing out of tune.
And mirrors can show me multiplied
many times, say, dressed up in red
or dressed up in grey.

Nobody can get into my clothes for me
or feel my fall for me, or do my running.
Nobody hears my music for me, either.

I am just this one.
Nobody else makes the words
I shape with sound, when I talk.

But anybody can act how I stutter in a rage.
Anybody can copy echoes I make.
And mirrors can show me multiplied
many times, say, dressed up in green
or dressed up in blue.

James Berry

Nothing Else

There's nothing I can't see
From here.

There's nothing I can't be
From here.

Because my eyes
Are open wide
To let the big
World come inside,

I think I can see me
From here.

Kit Wright

EXTRACT FROM **I Am the One**

I am the one whom ringdoves see
    Through chinks in boughs
    When they do not rouse
    In sudden dread,
But stay on cooing, as if they said:
    'Oh; it's only he.'

I am the passer when up-eared hares,
    Stirred as they eat
    The new-sprung wheat,
    Their munch resume
As if they thought: 'He is one for whom
    Nobody cares.'

Thomas Hardy

Friendship Poem

I'm a fish out of water
I'm two left feet
On my own and lonely
I'm incomplete

I'm boots without laces
I'm jeans without the zip
I'm lost, I'm a zombie
I'm a dislocated hip.

Roger McGough

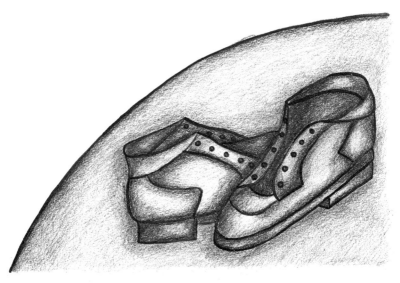

'I Am Cherry Alive,' the Little Girl Sang

'I am cherry alive,' the little girl sang,
'Each morning I am something new:
I am apple, I am plum, I am just as excited
As the boys who made the Hallowe'en bang:
I am tree, I am cat, I am blossom too:
When I like, if I like, I can be someone new,
Someone very old, a witch in a zoo:
I can be someone else whenever I think who,
And I want to be everything sometimes too:
And the peach has a pit and I know that too,
And I put it in along with everything
To make the grown-ups laugh whenever I sing:
And I sing: *It is true; it is untrue*:
I know, I know, the true is untrue,
The peach has a pit, the pit has a peach:
And both may be wrong when I sing my song,
But I don't tell the grown-ups: because it is sad,
And I want them to laugh just like I do
Because they grew up and forgot what they
    knew
And they are sure I will forget it some day too.
They are wrong. They are wrong. When I
    sang my song, I knew, I knew!
I am red, I am gold, I am green, I am blue,
I will always be me, I will always be new!'

Delmore Schwartz

Silent, But

I may be silent, but
I'm thinking.
I may not talk, but
Don't mistake me for a wall.

Tsuboi Shigeji

Tall Thots

It's quite nice
being small,
I don't really
mind at
all.
People don't pick
on you,
or beat you
up.
They even
listen to
you.
But I wish
I was taller,
then I could
get into a
AA film
with no questions asked.

Deepak Kalha

Growing Up?

It must be
a month or more
since they complained
about the way I eat

or crisps dropped
on the kitchen floor

or not washing my feet

or the TV left blaring
when I go out

or how loudly I shout

or my unmade bed
or mud on the stair

or the soap left to drown
or the state of my hair . . .

It *must* be
a month or more.
Have they given up
in despair?

For years they've
nagged me,
told me to grow up
and act my age.

Has it happened?
Am I now
about to step
onto the stage?

Wes Magee

Dumb Insolence

I'm big for ten years old
Maybe that's why they get at me

Teachers, parents, cops
Always getting at me

When they get at me

I don't hit em
They can do you for that

I don't swear at em
They can do you for that

I stick my hands in my pockets
And stare at them

And while I stare at them
I think about sick

They call it dumb insolence

They don't like it
But they can't do you for it

Adrian Mitchell

Sally

She was a dog-rose kind of girl:
elusive, scattery as petals;
scratchy sometimes, tripping you like briars.
She teased the boys
twisting this way and that, not to be tamed
or taught any more than the wind.
Even in school the word 'ought'
had no meaning for Sally.
On dull days
she'd sit quiet as a mole at her desk
delving in thought.
But when the sun called
she was gone, running the blue day down
till the warm hedgerows prickled the dusk
and the moths flickered out.

Her mother scolded; Dad
gave her the hazel-switch,
said her head was stuffed with feathers
and a starling tongue.
But they couldn't take the shine out of her.
Even when it rained
you felt the sun saved under her skin.
She'd a way of escape
laughing at you from the bright end of a tunnel,
leaving you in the dark.

Phoebe Hesketh

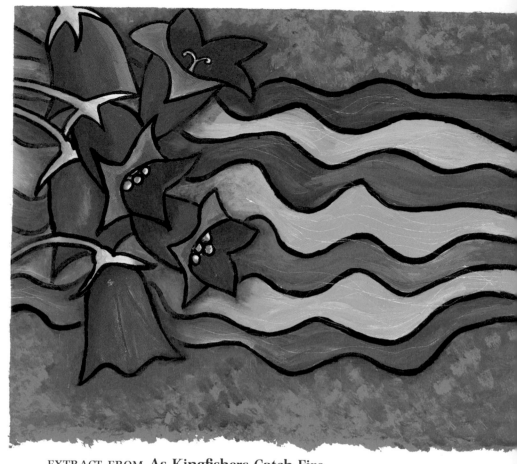

EXTRACT FROM **As Kingfishers Catch Fire**

As kingfishers catch fire, dragonflies draw flame;
    As tumbled over rim in roundy wells
    Stones ring; like each tucked string tells, each hung bell's
Bow swung finds tongue to fling out broad its name;
Each mortal thing does one thing and the same:
    Deals out that being indoors each one dwells;
    Selves – goes itself; *myself* it speaks and spells,
Crying *What I do is me: for that I came.*

Gerard Manley Hopkins

When I Went to the New School

When I went to the new school
people noticed I was a Jew.

I was the only one.

So they did the jokes:
you know,

throwing a penny on the floor
to see if I'd pick it up

rubbing their noses

going 'my boy' and 'my life'
while they were talking to me.

And if ever I had to borrow any money
there'd be uproar,
cheering, jeering,
'Don't lend him any money, you'll never get it back.'

Sometimes I'd go along with it
and I'd put on what I thought was
a Jewish voice
and say things like
'Nice bit of schmutter.'

It's like I was bringing Zaida
my mother's Dad, into the playground
running round him going,
'You're a Jew, you're a Jew.'

It's like I was saying
'Yes, I'm a Jew
but I'm not like other Jews,
I'm an OK-Jew.'

But I wasn't.
For them I was just
Jew.

I was the Jew that it was
OK-to-say-all-the-foul-things-
you-want-to-say-about-Jews-to.

And I played along with it,
I thought it'd stop them hating me
but all it did
was make it easier for them
to hate all Jews.

Michael Rosen

In-a Brixtan Markit

I walk in-a Brixtan markit,
believin I a respectable man,
you know. An wha happn?

Policeman come straight up
an search mi bag!
Man—straight to mi.
Like them did a-wait fi mi.
Come search mi bag, man.

Fi mi bag!
And wha them si in deh?
Two piece a yam, a dasheen,
a han a banana, a piece of pork
an mi lates Bob Marley.

Man all a sudden I feel
mi head nah fi mi. This yah now
is when man kill somody, nah!

'Tony,' I sey, 'hol on. Hol on,
Tony, Dohn shove. Dohn shove.
Dohn move neidda fis, tongue
nor emotion. Battn down, Tony.
Battn down.' An, man, Tony win.

James Berry

Acquainted with the Night

I have been one acquainted with the night.
I have walked out in rain – and back in rain.
I have outwalked the furthest city light.

I have looked down the saddest city lane.
I have passed by the watchman on his beat
And dropped my eyes, unwilling to explain.

I have stood still and stopped the sound of feet
When far away an interrupted cry
Came over houses from another street,

But not to call me back or say good-by;
And further still at an unearthly height,
One luminary clock against the sky

Proclaimed the time was neither wrong nor right.
I have been one acquainted with the night.

Robert Frost

I Have Lived and I Have Loved

I have lived and I have loved;
I have waked and I have slept;
I have sung and I have danced;
I have smiled and I have wept;
I have won and wasted treasure;
I have had my fill of pleasure;
And all these things were weariness,
And some of them were dreariness.
And all these things – but two things
Were emptiness and pain:
And Love – it was the best of them;
And Sleep – worth all the rest of them.

Anon

Requiem

Under the wide and starry sky,
　Dig the grave and let me lie.
Glad did I live and gladly die,
　And I laid me down with a will.

This be the verse you grave for me:
Here he lies where he longed to be;
Home is the sailor, home from the sea,
　And the hunter home from the hill.

Robert Louis Stevenson

It's a Mad, Mad World

Recipe

Take a roof of old tiles
shortly after midday.

Place all beside
a full-grown linden
stirred by the wind.

Put over them
a blue sky washed
by some white clouds.

Leave them alone.
Look at them.

Guillevic

Bush-warbler

A bush-warbler
Coming to the verandah-edge,
Left its droppings
On the rice-cakes.

Matsuo Basho

Snail

Slowly, slowly climb
Up and up Mount Fiji,
O snail.

Kobayashi Issa

Wild Geese

Beating their wings
Against the white clouds
You can count each one
Of the wild geese flying:
Moon, an autumn night.

Traditional, Japan

Caterpillar's Lullaby

Your sleep will be
a lifetime
and all your dreams
rainbows.
Close your eyes
and spin yourself
a fairy tale:
Sleeping Ugly,
Waking Beauty.

Jane Yolen

Leaf-eater

On a shrub in the heart of the garden,
On an outer leaf, a grub twists
Half its body, a tendril,
This way and that in blind
Space: no leaf or twig
Anywhere in reach; then gropes
Back on itself and begins
To eat its own leaf.

Thomas Kinsella

The Fly

The Fly
Is the Sanitary Inspector. He detects every speck
With his Geiger counter.
Detects it, then inspects it
Through his multiple spectacles. You see him everywhere
Bent over his microscope.

He costs nothing, needs no special attention,
Just gets on with the job, totting up the dirt.

All he needs is a lick of sugar
Maybe a dab of meat –
Which is fuel for his apparatus.
We never miss what he asks for. He can manage
With so little you can't even tell
Whether he's taken it.

In his black boiler suit, with his gas-mask,
His oxygen pack,
His crampons,
He can get anywhere, explore any wreckage,
Find the lost –

Whatever dies – just leave it to him.
He'll move in
With his team of gentle undertakers,
In their pneumatic protective clothing, afraid of nothing,
Little white Michelin men,

They hoover up the rot, the stink, and the goo.
He'll leave you the bones and the feathers – souvenirs
Dry-clean as dead sticks in the summer dust.

Panicky people misunderstand him —
Blitz at him with nerve-gas puff-guns,
Blot him up with swatters.

He knows he gets filthy.
He knows his job is dangerous, wading in the drains
Under cows' tails, in pigs' eye-corners
And between the leaky broken toes
Of the farm buildings —
He too has to cope with the microbes.
He too wishes he had some other job.

But this is his duty.
Just let him be. Let him rest on the wall there,
Scrubbing the back of his neck. This is his rest-minute.

Once he's clean, he's a gem.

A freshly barbered sultan, royally armoured
In dusky rainbow metals.

A knight on a dark horse.

Ted Hughes

How Everything Happens
(BASED ON A STUDY OF THE WAVE)

                                               happen.
                                          to
                                     up
                              stacking
                         is
                  something
When nothing is happening

When it happens
            something
                 pulls
                     back
                       not
                         to
                           happen.
When   has happened.
      pulling back   stacking up
           happens

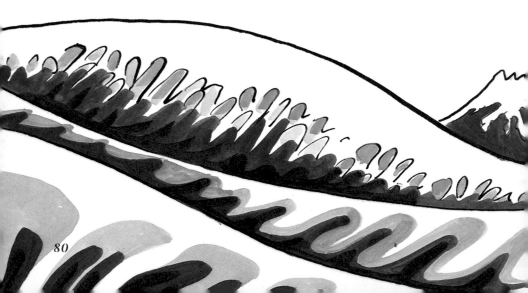

                    has happened   stacks up.
When it   something   nothing
                        pulls back while

Then nothing is happening.
                                        happens.
                            and
                    forward
                pushes
            up
        stacks
    something
Then

May Swenson

Sir Henry Morgan's Song

we came to the boat and blew the horn
we blew the boom and came to the island
we came the innocent and cut the cackle
we cut the tackle and stripped the bosun
we stripped the brandy and shaved the parrot
we shaved the part and shut the trap
we shut the shroud and bent the log
we bent the ocean and swung the lead
we swung the lumber and blued the lamp
we blued the thunder and crawled the crazes
we crawled Mither Carey and came to St Elmo
we came to the Horn and blew the boat

Edwin Morgan

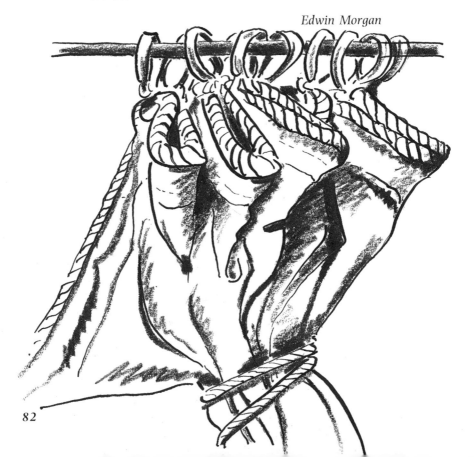

Sun a-Shine, Rain a-Fall

Sun a-shine an' rain a-fall,
The Devil an' him wife cyan 'gree at all,
The two o' them want one fish-head,
The Devil; call him wife bonehead,
She hiss her teeth, call him cock-eye,
Greedy, worthless an' workshy,
While them busy callin' name,
The puss walk in, sey is a shame
To see a nice fish go to was'e,
Lef' with a big grin 'pon him face.

Valerie Bloom

Rain and Sun

Rain falling, sun shining
The devil and his wife
Behind the church fighting

Odette Thomas

Autumn

And it is all over.

No more sweetpeas,
no more wide-eyed bunnies
dropping from the sky.

Only
a reddish boniness
under the sun of hoar frost,
a thievish fog,
an insipid solution of love,
        hate
        and craving.

But next year
larches will try
to make the land full of larches again
and larks will try
to make the land full of larks.

And thrushes will try
to make all the trees sing,
and goldfinches will try
to make all the grass golden,

and burying beetles
with their creaky love will try
to make all the corpses
rise from the dead,

Amen.

Miroslav Holub

Late Autumn Poem

birdless, and
almost bared,
Trees,
twigs chattering,
 squeeze the last drops
  out of the sun
    and rub them
     deep into parts
       only trees know about.

Roger McGough

85

It's Winter, it's Winter

It's winter, it's winter, it's wonderful winter,
When everyone lounges around in the sun!

It's winter, it's winter, it's wonderful winter,
When everyone's brown like a steak overdone!

It's winter, it's winter, it's wonderful winter,
It's swimming and surfing and hunting for conkers!

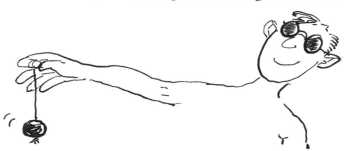

It's winter, it's winter, it's wonderful winter,
And I am completely and utterly bonkers!

Kit Wright

'Twas Midnight

'Twas midnight on the ocean,
Not a streetcar was in sight,
The sun was shining brightly,
For it rained all day that night.
'Twas a summer day in winter
And snow was raining fast
As a barefoot boy with shoes on
Stood sitting on the grass.

Anon

Kid Stuff

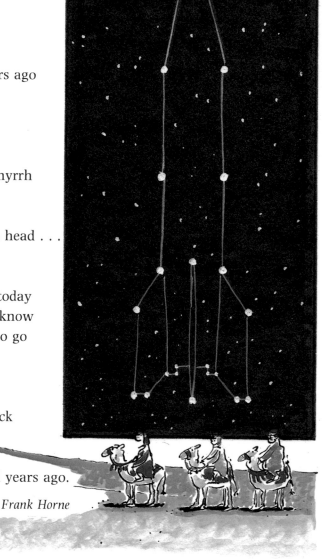

The wise guys
tell me
that Christmas
is Kid Stuff . . .
Maybe they've got
something there –
Two thousand years ago
three wise guys
chased a star
across a continent
to bring
frankincense and myrrh
to a Kid
born in a manger
with an idea in his head . . .
And as the bombs
crash
all over the world today
the real wise guys know
that we've all got to go
chasing stars
again
in the hope
that we can get back
some of that
Kid Stuff
born two thousand years ago.

Frank Horne

Reindeer Report

Chimneys: colder.
Flightpaths: busier.
Driver: Christmas (F)
Still baffled by postcodes.

Children: more
And stay up later.
Presents: heavier.
Pay: frozen.

Mission in spite
Of all this
Accomplished:

MERRY CHRISTMAS

U A Fanthorpe

Nothingmas Day

No it wasn't.

It was Nothingmas Eve and all the children in Notown were not
tingling with excitement as they lay unawake in their heaps.
D

  o

    w

      n

        s

          t

        a

          i

        r

            s their parents were busily not placing the last
crackermugs, glimmerslips and sweetlumps on the Nothingmas
Tree.

Hey! But what was that invisible trail of chummy sparks or
vaulting stars across the sky
    Father Nothingmas – drawn by 18 or 21
    rainmaidens!
    Father Nothingmas – his sackbut bulging with air!
    Father Nothingmas – was not on his way!
(From the streets of the snowless town came the quiet of
unsung carols and the merry silence of the steeple bell.)

Next morning the children did not fountain out of bed with cries
of WHOOPERATION! They picked up their Nothingmas
Stockings and with traditional quiperamas such as: 'Look what
I haven't got! It's just what I didn't want!' pulled their stockings
on their ordinary legs.

For breakfast they ate – breakfast.

After woods they all avoided the Nothingmas Tree, where Daddy, his face failing to beam like a leaky torch, was not distributing gemgames, sodaguns, golly-trolleys, jars of humdrums and packets of slubberated croakers.

Off, off, off went the children to school, soaking each other with no howls of 'Merry Nothingmas and a Happy No Year!', and not pulping each other with no-balls.

At school Miss Whatnot taught them how to write No Thank You Letters.

Home they burrowed for Nothingmas Dinner.
The table was not groaning under all manner of
    NO TURKEY
    NO SPICED HAM
    NO SPROUTS
    NO CRANBERRY JELLYSAUCE
    NO NOT NOWT
There was not one (1) shoot of glee as the Nothingmas Pudding, unlit, was not brought in. Mince pies were not available, nor was there any demand for them.

Then, as another Nothingmas clobbered to a close, they all haggled off to bed where they slept happily never after.

   and that is not the end of the story . . . .

Adrian Mitchell

Cowboy Movies

On cowboy movies
   they show you Indians as baddies
   and cowboys as goodies

but think again please;

   who disturb de dreams
      of de sleeping wigwam
      who come with de guns
         going blam blam blam?

Think again please.

John Agard

They Hang the Man

They hang the man and beat the woman
Who steal the goose from off the common
But let the greater villain loose
Who stole the common from the goose.

Traditional, England

A Child is Singing

A child is singing
And nobody listening
But the child who is singing:

Bulldozers grab the earth and shower it.
The house is on fire.
Gardeners wet the earth and flower it.
The house is on fire,
The houses are on fire.
Fetch the fire engine, the fire engine's on fire.
We will have to hide in a hole.
We will burn slow like coal.
All the people are on fire.

And a child is singing
And nobody listening
But the child who is singing.

Adrian Mitchell

The Fish are All Sick

The fish are all sick, the great whales dead,
The villages stranded in stone on the coast,
Ornamental, like pearls on the fringe of a coat.
Sea men, who knew what the ocean did,
Turned their low houses away from the surf.
But new men who come to be rural and safe
Add big glass views and begonia beds.
Water keeps to itself.
White lip after lip
Curls to a close on the littered beach.
Something is sicker and blacker than fish.
And closing its grip, and closing its grip.

Anne Stevenson

Nursery Rhyme

What do we use to wash our hair?
We use shampoo to wash our hair.
It's tested scientifically for damage to the eyes
by scientists who, in such matters, are acknowledged
to be wise.
Shampoo. Wash hair. Nice, clean habit.
Go to sleep now, darling.
It doesn't hurt the rabbit.

What makes lather in the bath tub?
Soap makes lather in the bath tub.
Rub-a-dub till bubbles bob along the rubber ducks race!
But don't get any in your mouth because soap has a
nasty taste.
Bath time. Slippy soap! Can't quite grab it!
Let's get dried now, darling.
It doesn't hurt the rabbit.

What makes us better when we're ill?
Medicine helps us when we're ill.
Years of research helped to develop every pill you take,
Like that one we gave you when you had a
tummy ache.
Cut knee. Antiseptic. Gently dab it.
Kiss you better, darling.
It doesn't hurt the rabbit.
It doesn't hurt
It doesn't hurt
It doesn't hurt the rabbit.

Carol Ann Duffy

Percy Pot-Shot

Percy Pot-Shot went out hunting,
Percy Pot-Shot and his gun,
Percy Pot-Shot, such a hot shot,
Shot a sparrow, said 'What fun!'

Percy Pot-Shot shot a blackbird,
Shot a lapwing, shot a duck,
Shot a swan as it rose flapping,
Shot an eagle, said 'What luck!'

Percy Pot-Shot shot a rabbit,
Shot a leaping, gold-eyed hare,
Shot a tiger that lay sleeping,
Shot a rhino, shot a bear.

Percy Pot-Shot, trigger happy,
Shot a fountain, shot a tree,
Shot a river, shot a mountain,
Shot some rainclouds, shot the sea.

Percy Pot-Shot went on hunting,
Percy Pot-Shot and his gun,
Not a lot that he had not shot,
Shot the moon down, shot the sun.

Percy Pot-Shot stood in darkness,
No bird fluttered, no beast stirred,
Percy Pot-Shot knelt and muttered
'God forgive me.' No one heard.

Richard Edwards

Extinction Day

The Dodo and the Barbary Lion,
The Cuban Yellow Bat,
The Atlas Bear, the Quagga and
The Christmas Island Rat,
The Thylacine, the Blue Buck
And the Hau Kuahiwi plant
Have all one thing in common now,
And that is that they aren't.

Give me one good reason why,
I wonder if you can?
The answer's in a single word –
The word is simply: Man.

Extinction Day, Extinction Day,
It isn't all that far away
For many animals and birds.
So let us decimate the herds,
Let's hunt their eggs and spoil their land,
Let's give Extinction a Big Hand,
For when it comes, it's here to stay . . .
Extinction Day! Extinction Day!

Terry Jones

Acknowledgements

'$' by Carol Ann Duffy from *Standing Female Nude*, Anvil Press Poetry 1985; 'I'm a Hip Hoppy Kid' from *Wither and Chips*, Fleetway Publications; 'Well Listen' by permission of the author; 'Beat Drummers' by Benjamin Zephaniah from *The Dread Affair* by permission of Century Hutchinson; extract from 'Drums' by Lari Williams from *Drumcall*, Barbican Books 1971; extract from 'Didn't He Ramble' by Edward Kamau Brathwaite from *The Arrivants*, Oxford University Press 1975, reprinted by permission of Oxford University Press; 'What the Wind Said' by Russell Hoban from *The Pedalling Man*, William Heinemann Ltd; 'A Minor Bird' by Robert Frost from *Collected Poems*, edited by Edward Connery Latham, Jonathan Cape 1943, reprinted by permission of the Estate of Robert Frost and from *The Poetry of Robert Frost* edited by Edward Connery Latham. Copyright 1928, © 1969 by Holt, Rinehart and Winston. Copyright © 1956 by Robert Frost. Reprinted by permission of Henry Holt and Company, Inc.; 'I Cannot Give the Reasons' by Mervyn Peake from *A Book of Nonsense*, Peter Owen Ltd; 'Song for a Banjo Dance' by Langston Hughes from *The Weary Blues*, Alfred A Knopf Inc 1926; 'Drum Feet' by Mike Taylor, by permission of the author; 'Black Bottom' by Jackie Kay, by permission of the author; 'When I Dance' by James Berry from *When I Dance*, Hamish Hamilton Ltd, London 1988 © James Berry, 1988, reproduced by permission of Hamish Hamilton Ltd; 'Happiness' from *Selected Poems* by Günther Grass © 1966 Martin Secker and Warburg Ltd, reprinted by permission of Martin Secker and Warburg Ltd; 'The One About Fred Astaire' by Adrian Mitchell by permission of the author; Bogle L'Ouverture Publications for 'Klassical Dub' from *Dread Beat and Blood* by Linton Kwesi Johnson, published 1975; 'Break/dance' © Grace Nichols, by permission of Grace Nichols.

'Me and the Mule' by Langston Hughes, copyright 1942 by Alfred A Knopf Inc and renewed 1970 by Arna Bontemps & George Houston Bass, reprinted from *Selected Poems of Langston Hughes* by permission of Alfred A Knopf Inc; 'Before and After' and 'When I Went to the New School' from *When Did You Last Wash Your Feet?* by Michael Rosen, André Deutsch, 1986; 'Conversation with Myself' by Eve Merriam from *A Sky Full of Poems*. Copyright © 1964, 1970, 1973 by Eve Merriam. Reprinted by permission of Marian Reiner for the author; 'One' by James Berry from *When I Dance* by James Berry, Hamish Hamilton, 1988, London, © James Berry 1988, reproduced by permission of Hamish Hamilton Ltd; 'Nothing Else' by Kit Wright, from *Cat Among the Pigeons* by Kit Wright (Viking Kestrel, 1988) copyright © Kit Wright, 1988; 'Friendship Poem' from *Sky in the Pie* by Roger McGough, reprinted by permission of the Peters Fraser & Dunlop Group Ltd; '"I am Cherry Alive", the Little Girl Sang' by Delmore Schwartz from *Selected Poems: Summer Knowledge* copyright © 1959 by Delmore Schwartz, reprinted by permission of Laurence Pollinger and New Directions Publishing Corp; 'Silent, but' from *The Penguin Book of Japanese Verse*, translated by G Bownas and A Thwaite (Penguin Books, 1964), translation © G Bownas and A Thwaite, 1964, reproduced by permission of Penguin Books; 'Growing Up?' from *Morning Break* by Wes Magee, Cambridge University Press, 1989, by permission of the author; 'Dumb Insolence' from *Nothingmas Day* by Adrian Mitchell, Allison & Busby, 1984, by permission of the author; 'Sally' by Phoebe Hesketh from *Song of Sunlight*, The Bodley Head; 'In-a Brixtan Markit' from *Chain of Days* by James Berry, Oxford University Press, 1985, reprinted by permission of Oxford University Press; 'Acquainted with the Night' from *The Poetry of Robert Frost*, edited by Edward Connery Lathem, copyright 1928, © 1969 by Holt, Rinehart and Winston, copyright © 1956 by Robert Frost. Reprinted by permission of Henry Holt and Company, Inc.

'Recipe' from *Selected Poems of Guillevic*, translated by T Savory, Penguin, 1974, from the original 'Recette' from *Avec* by Eugène Guillevic © Éditions Gallimard 1966; 'A Bush-warbler' from *The Narrow Road to the Deep North and Other Travel Sketches* by Basho, translated by Nobuyuki Yuasa

101

Index of first lines